This Coloring Book
belongs to :

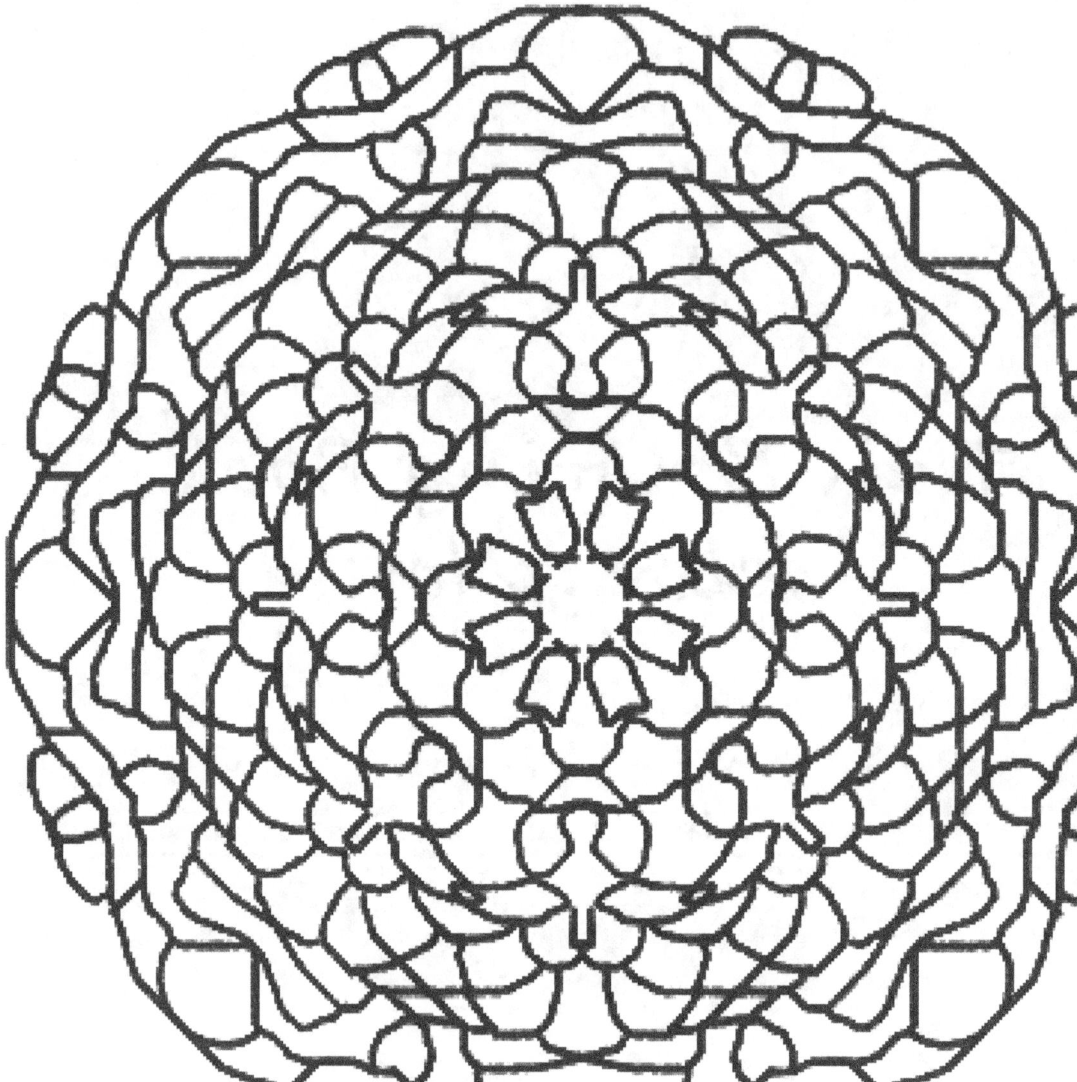

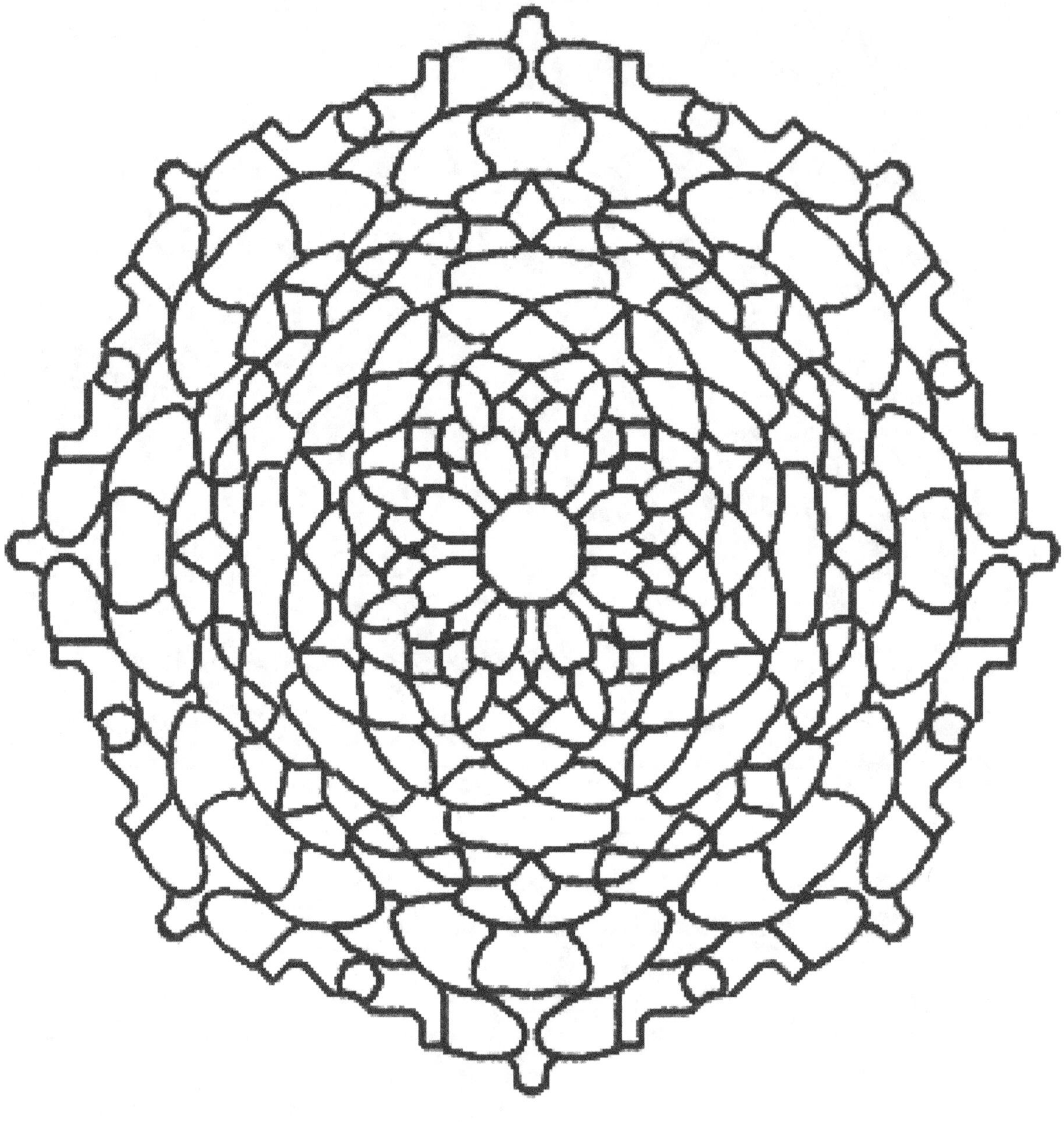

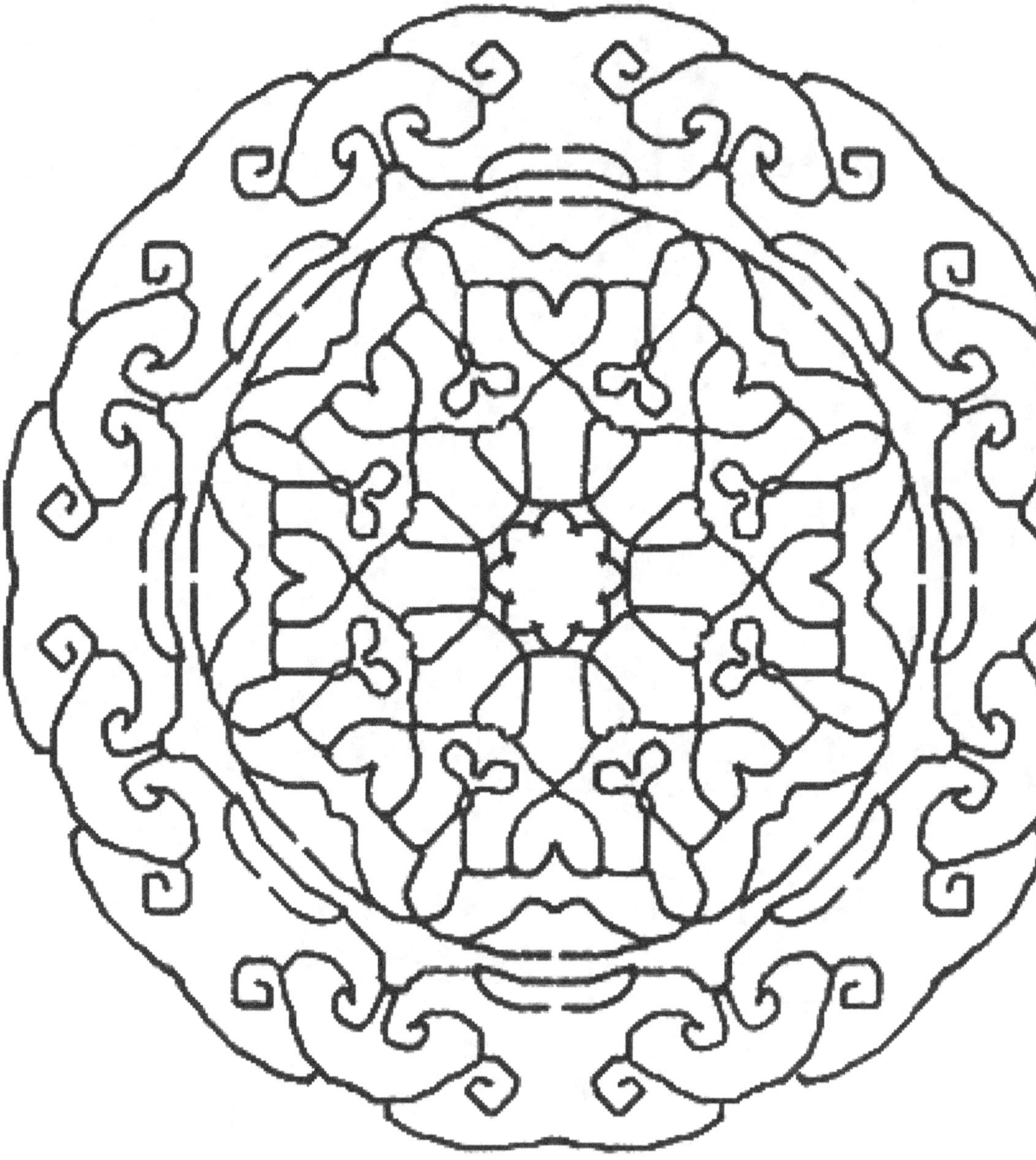

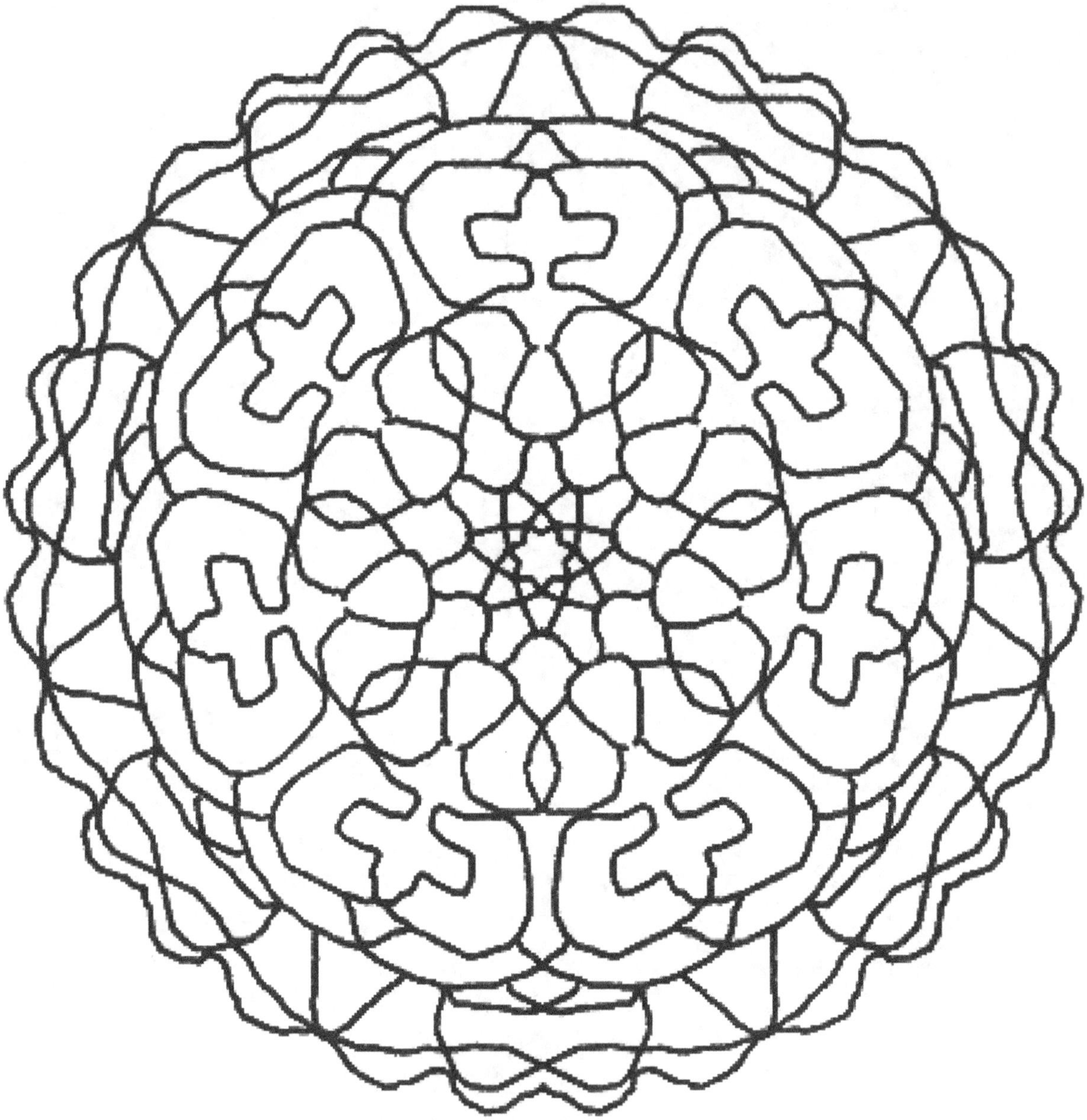

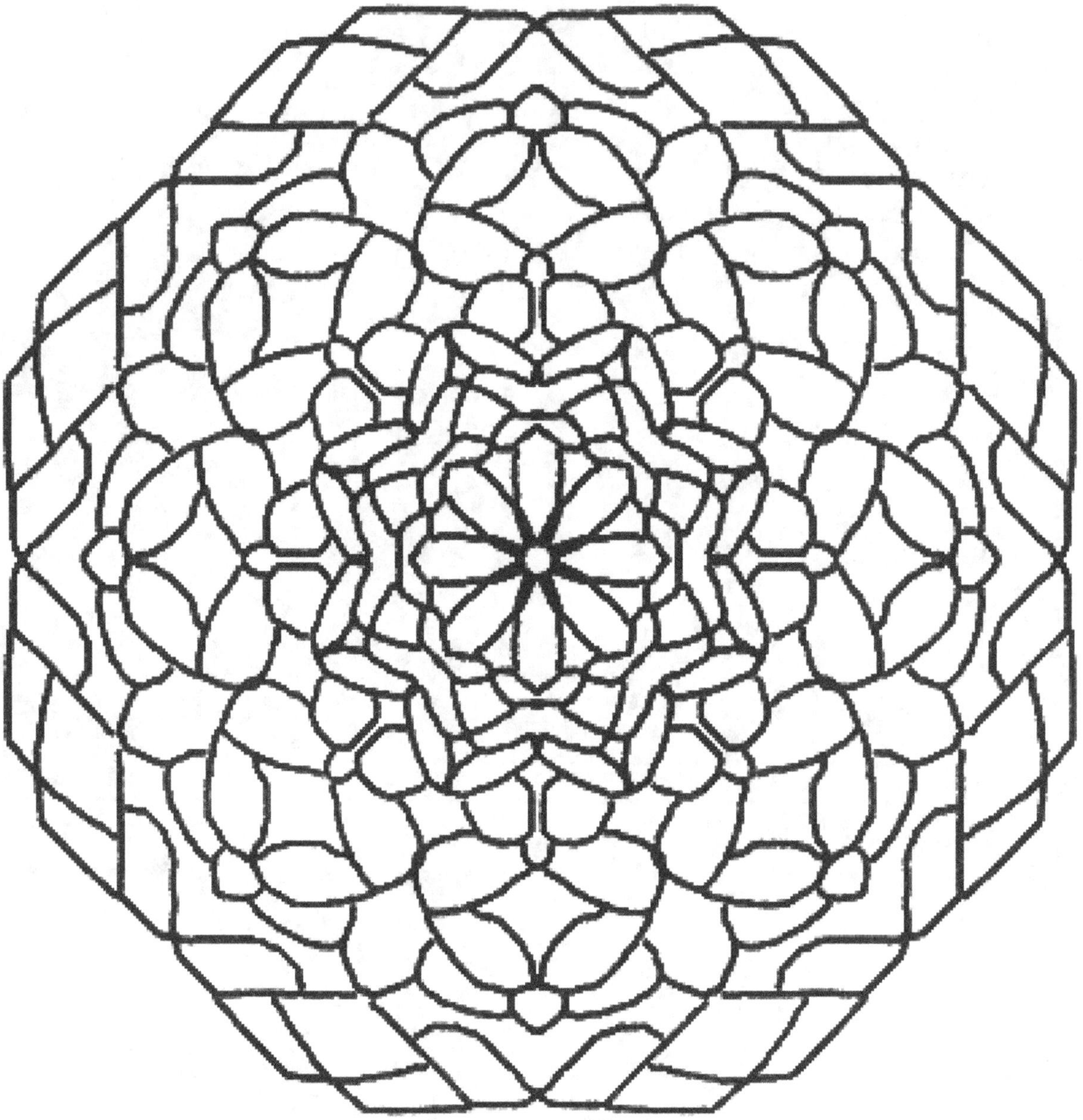

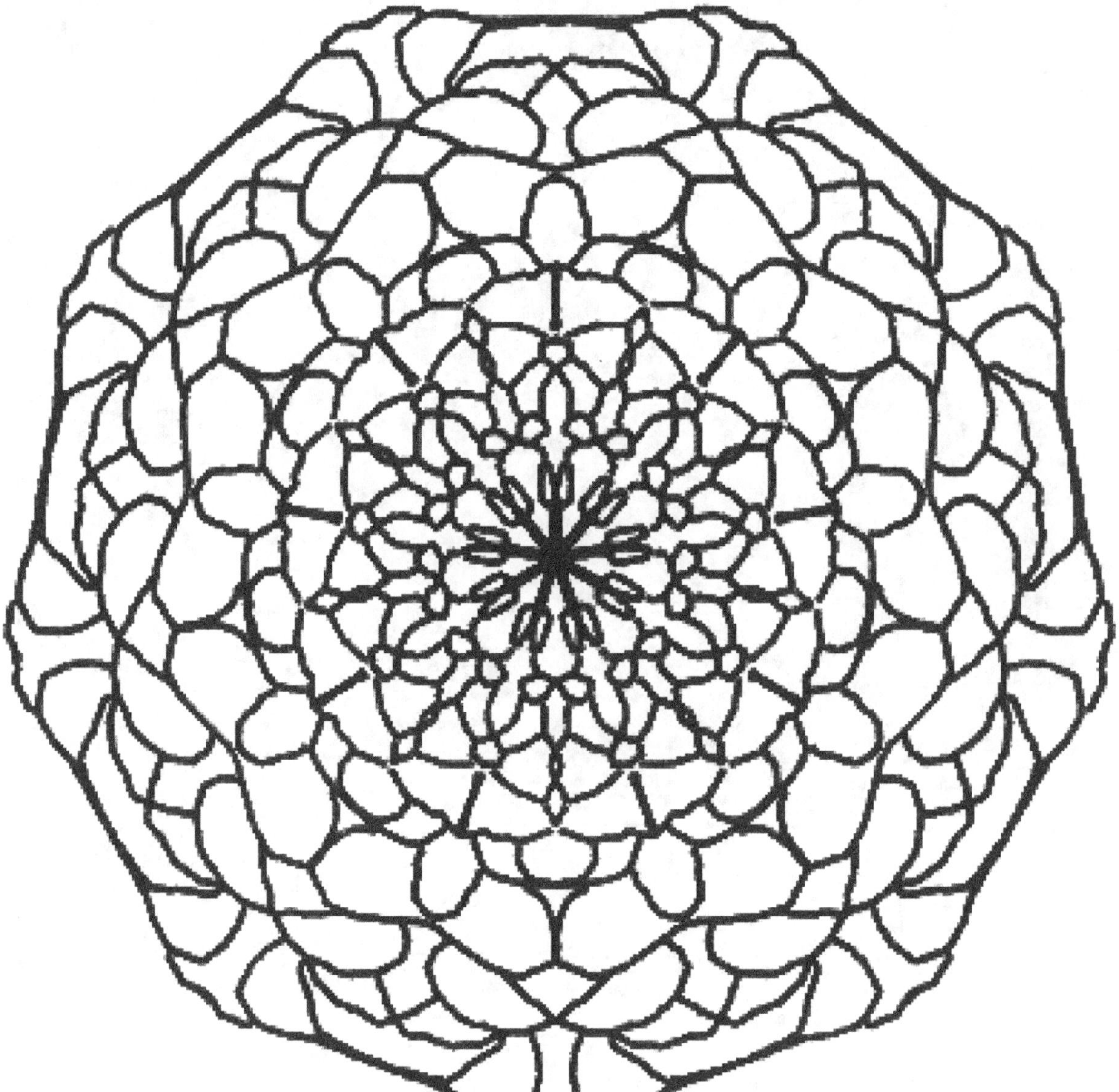

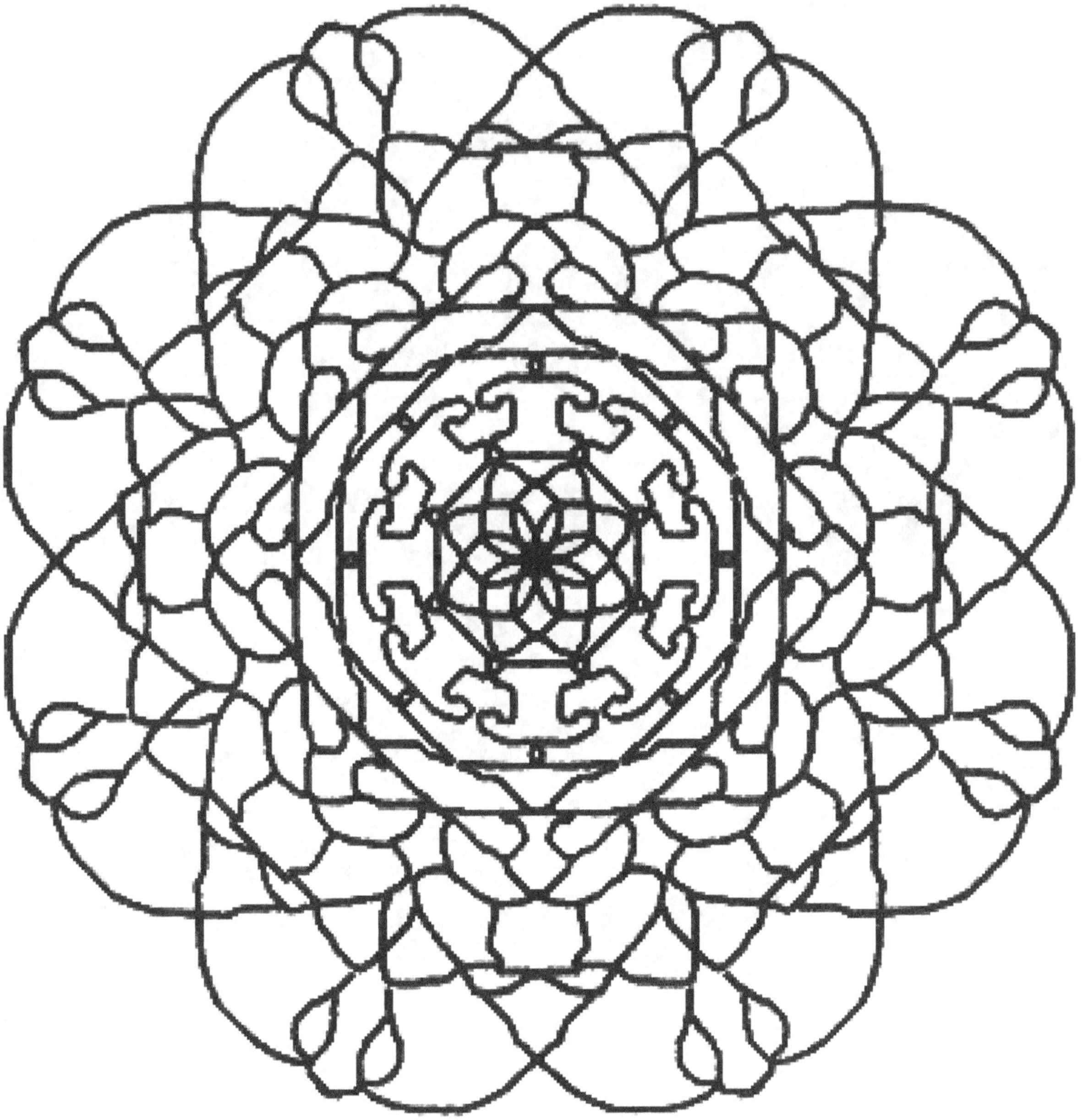

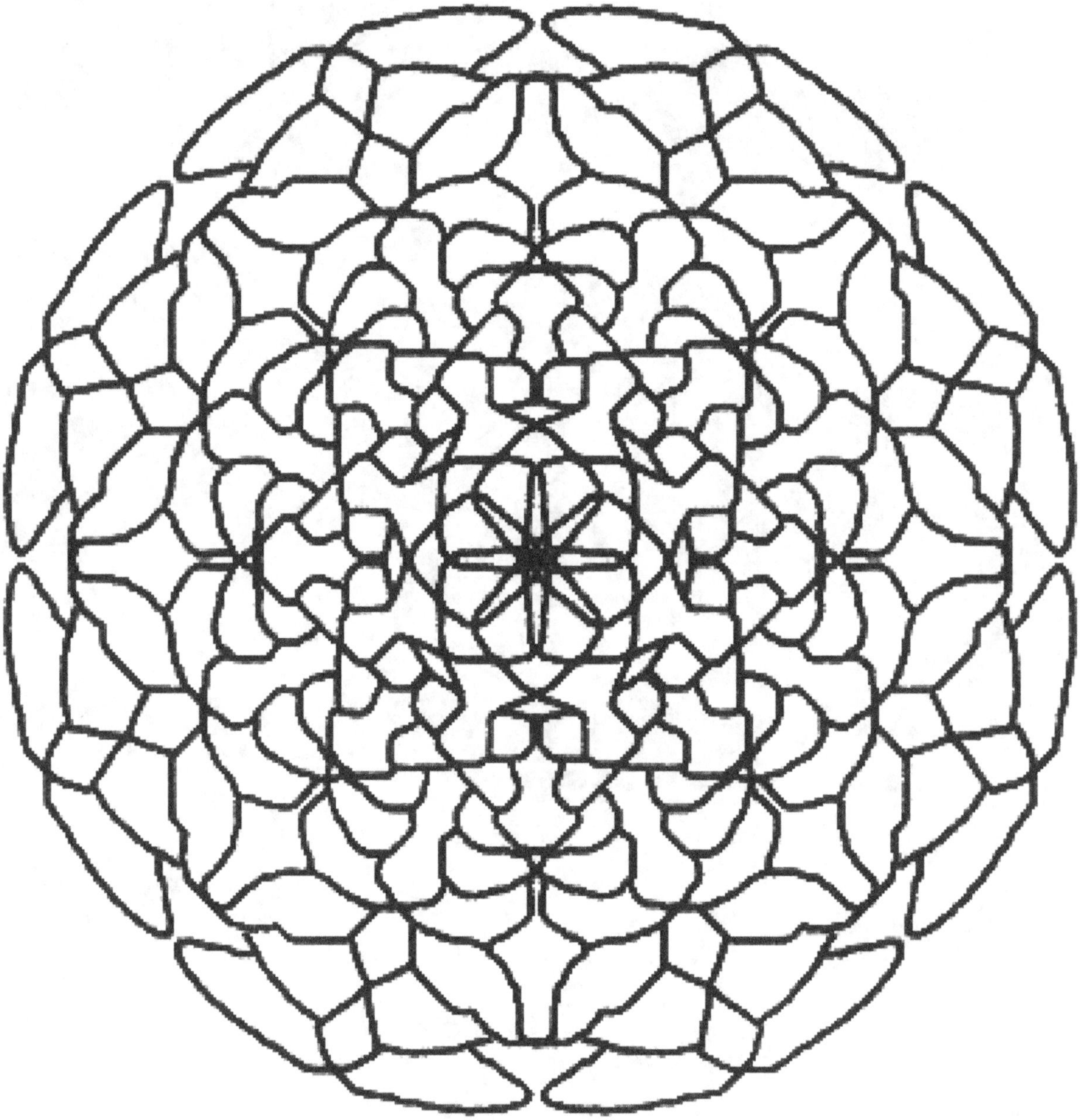

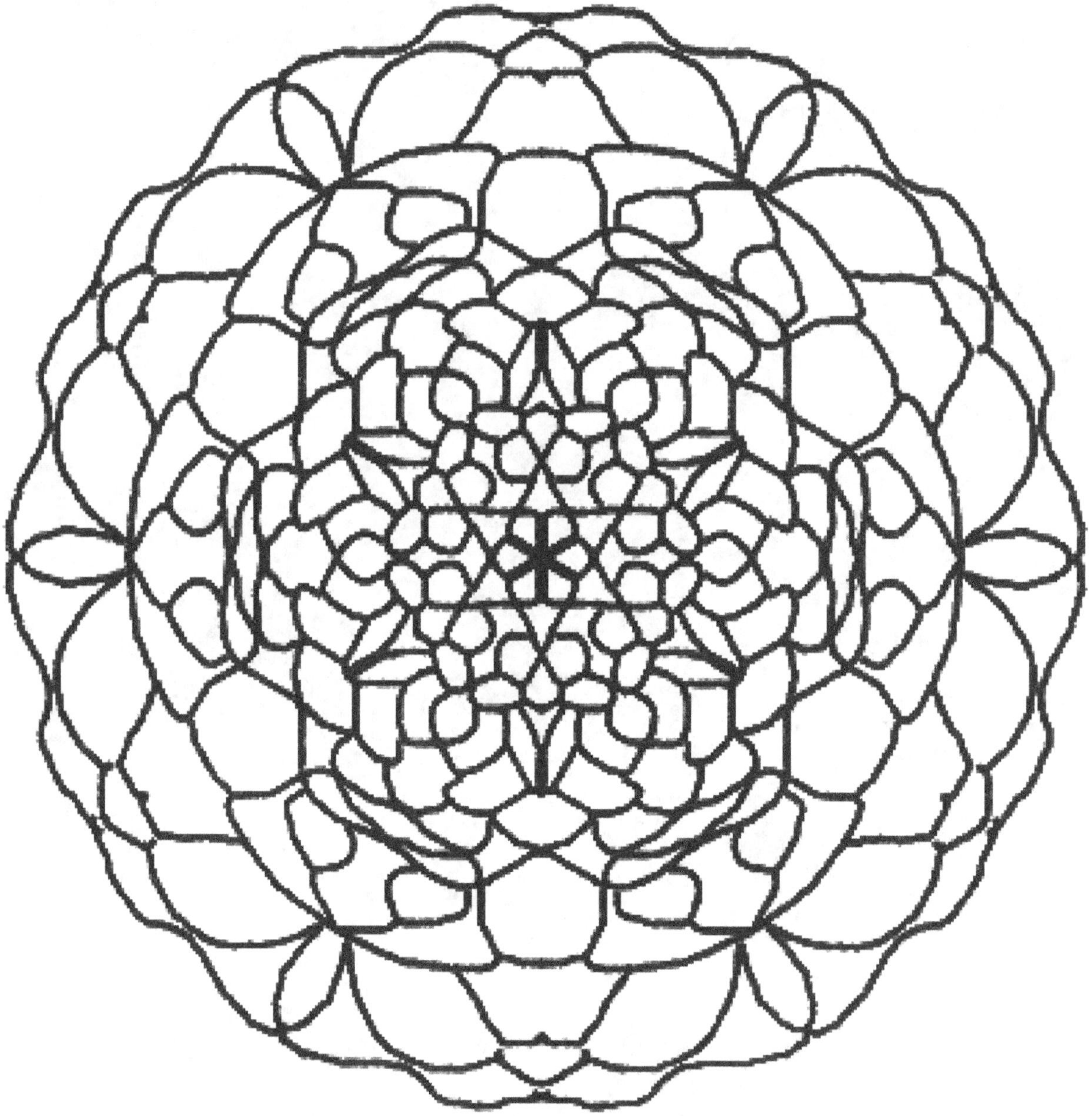

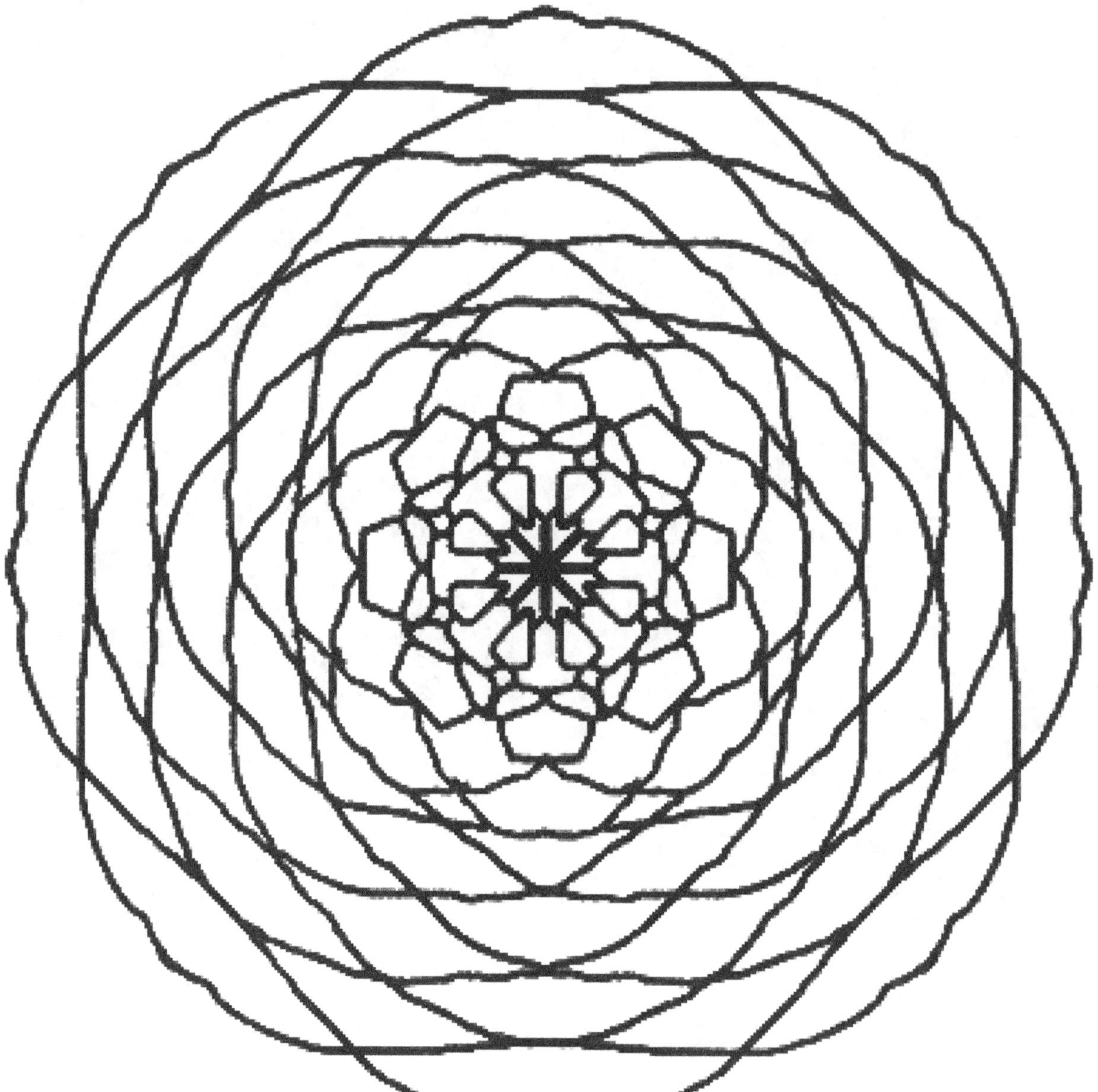

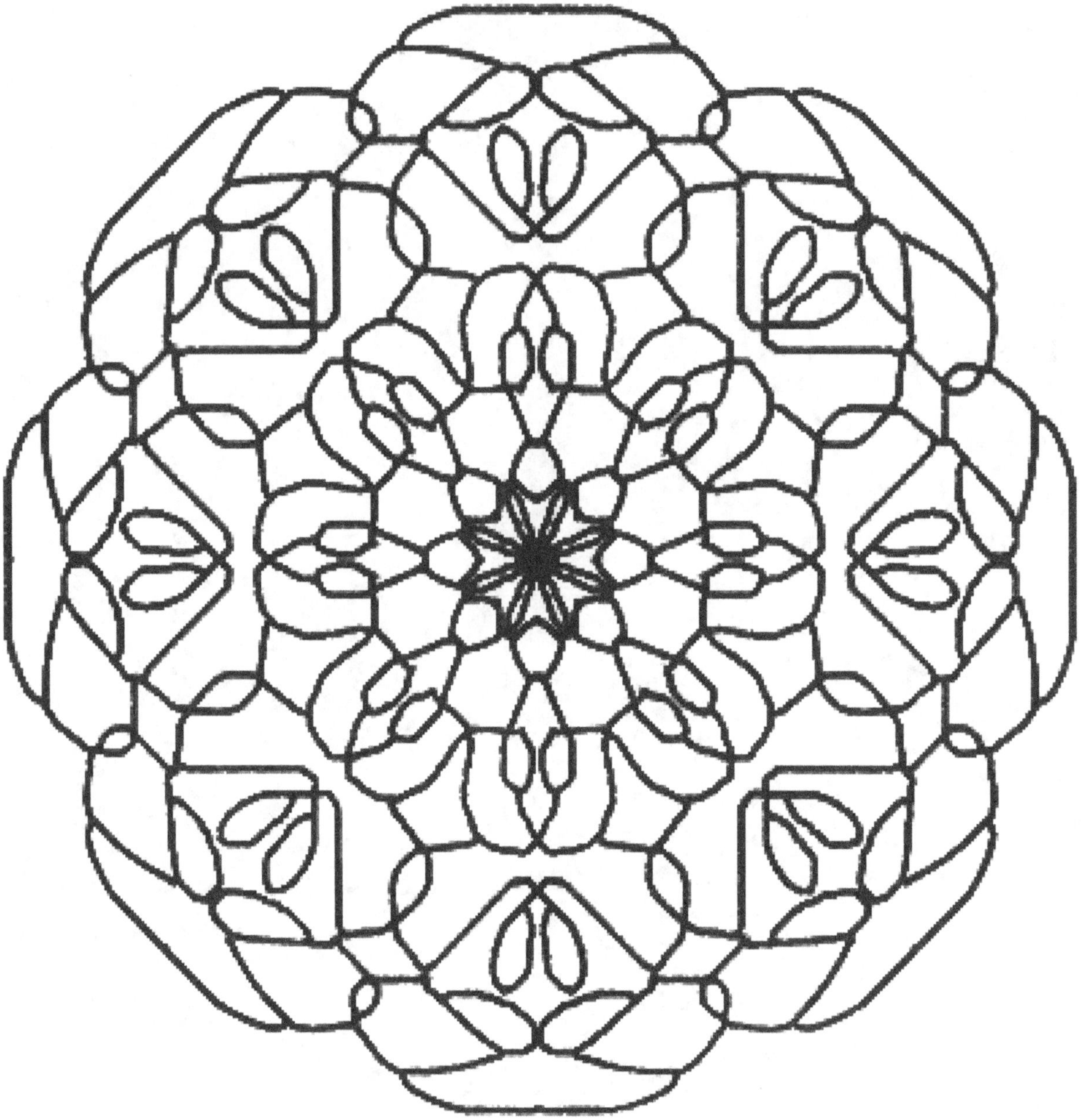

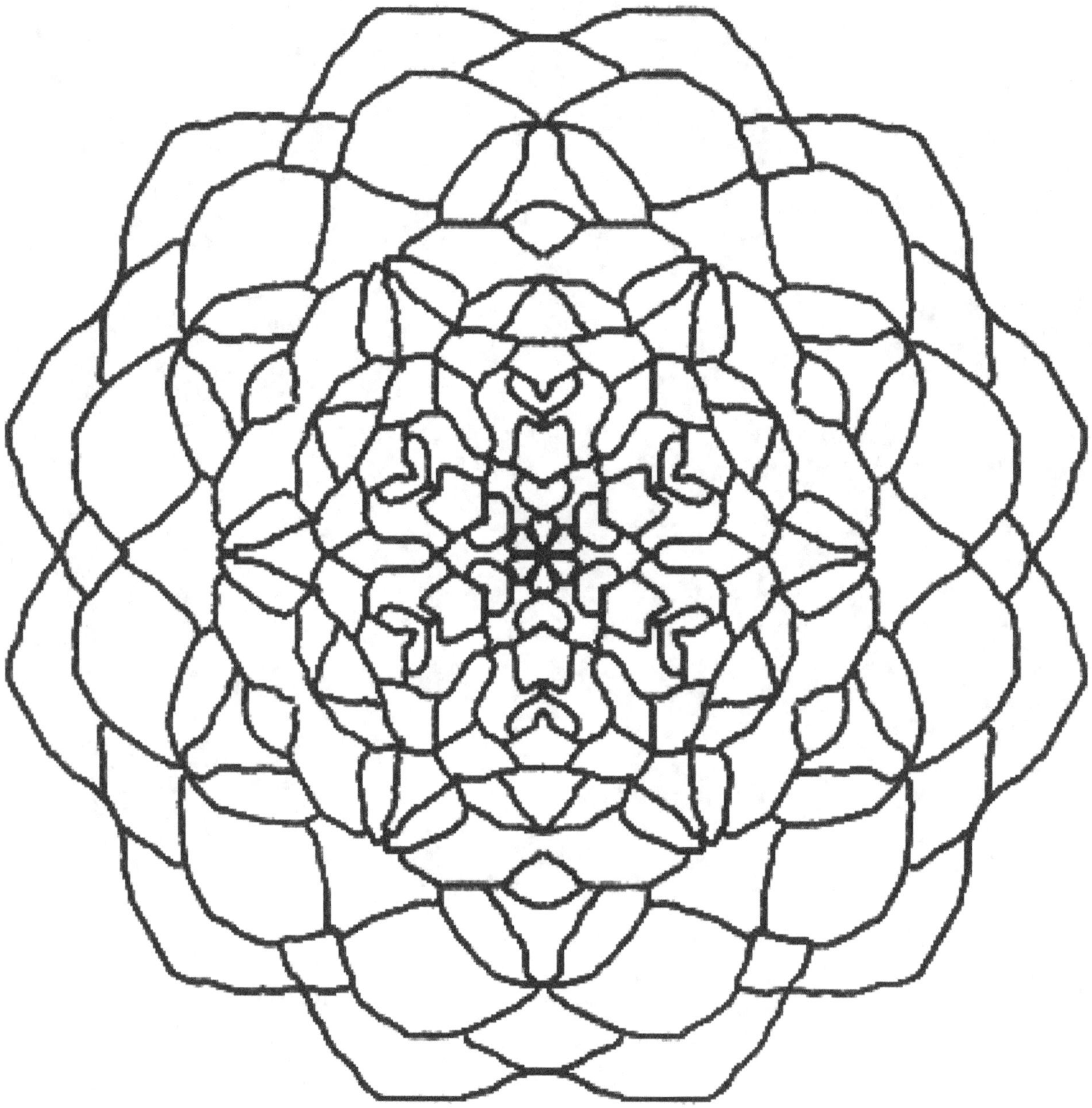

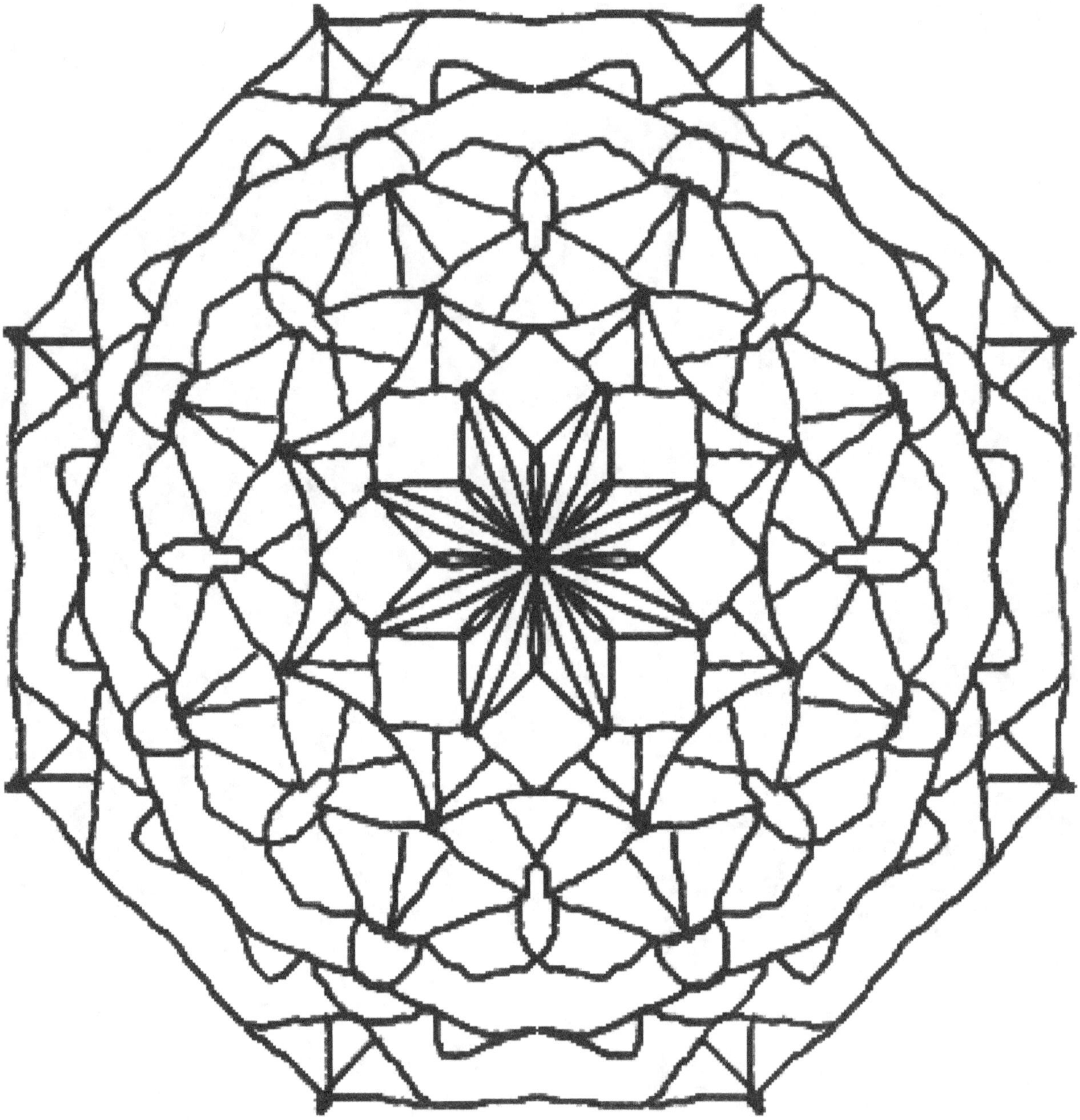

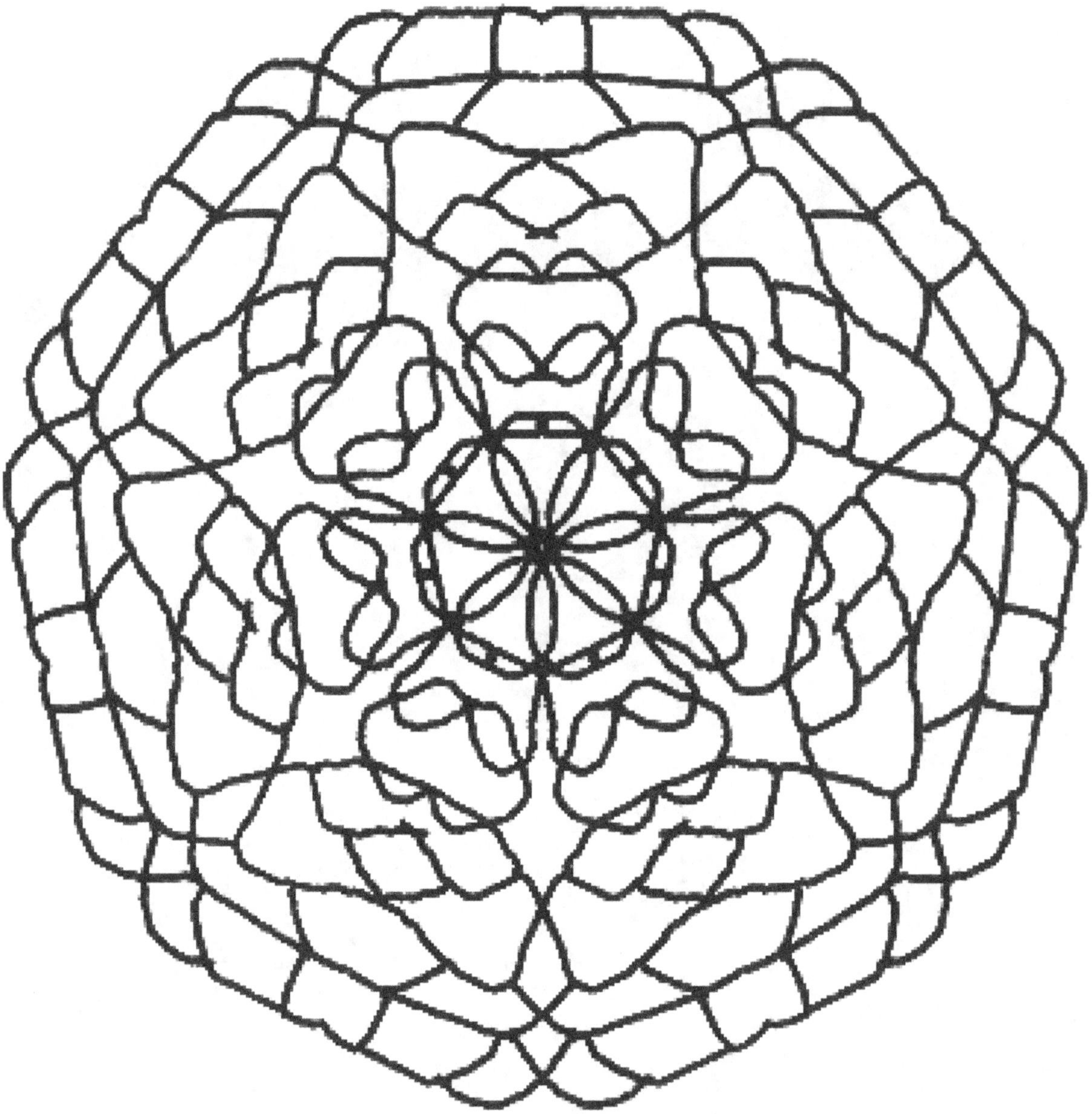

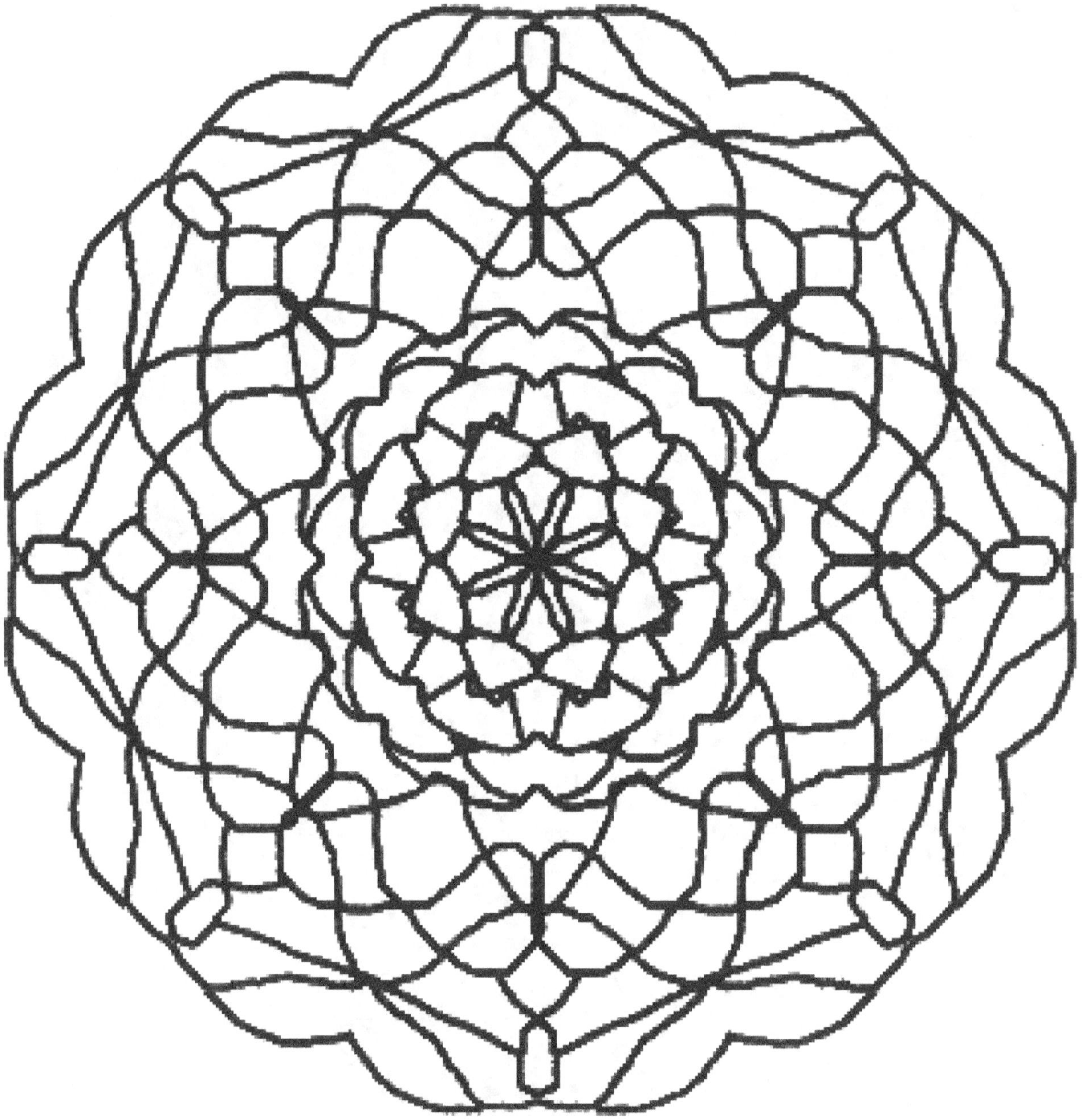

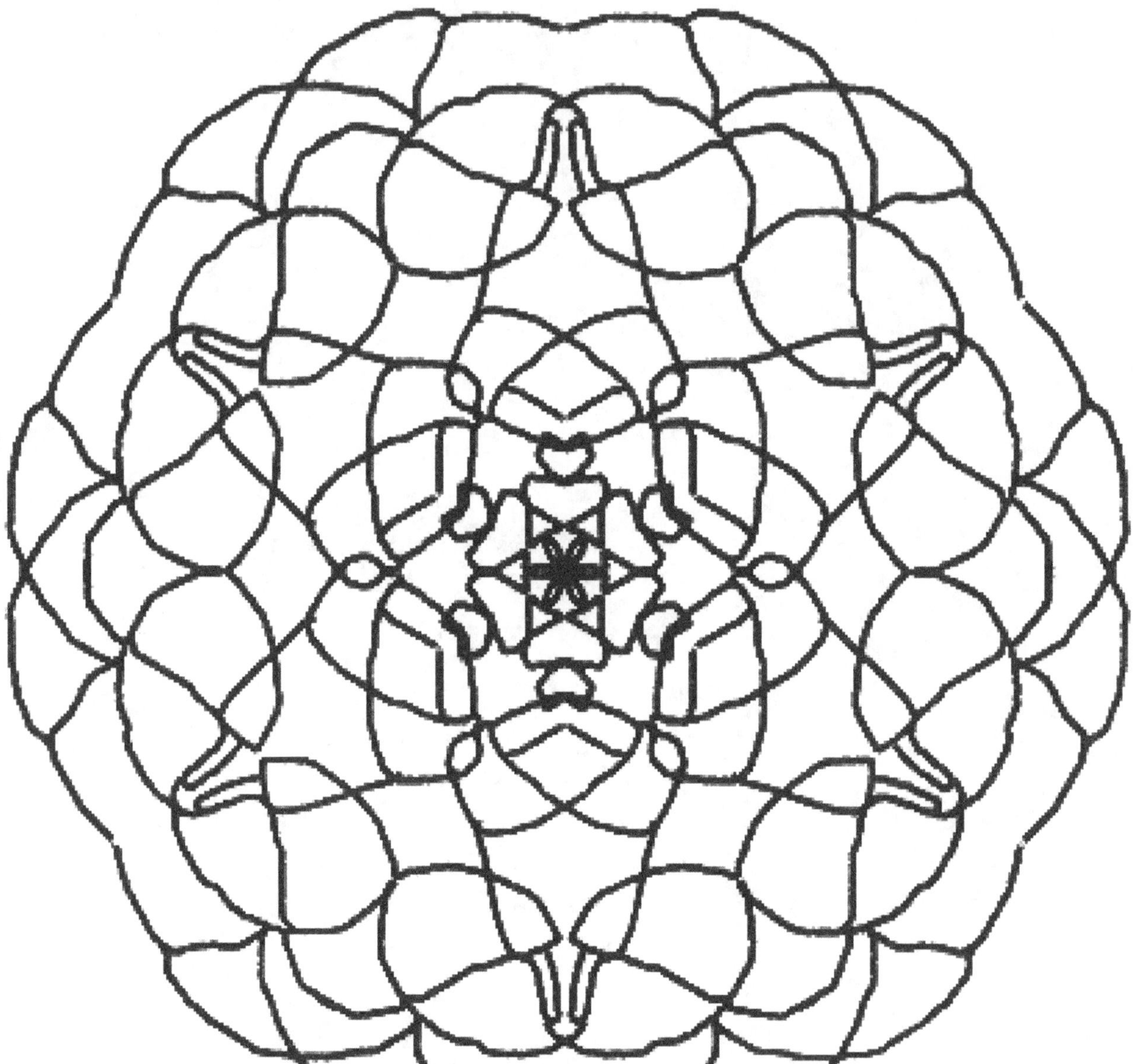

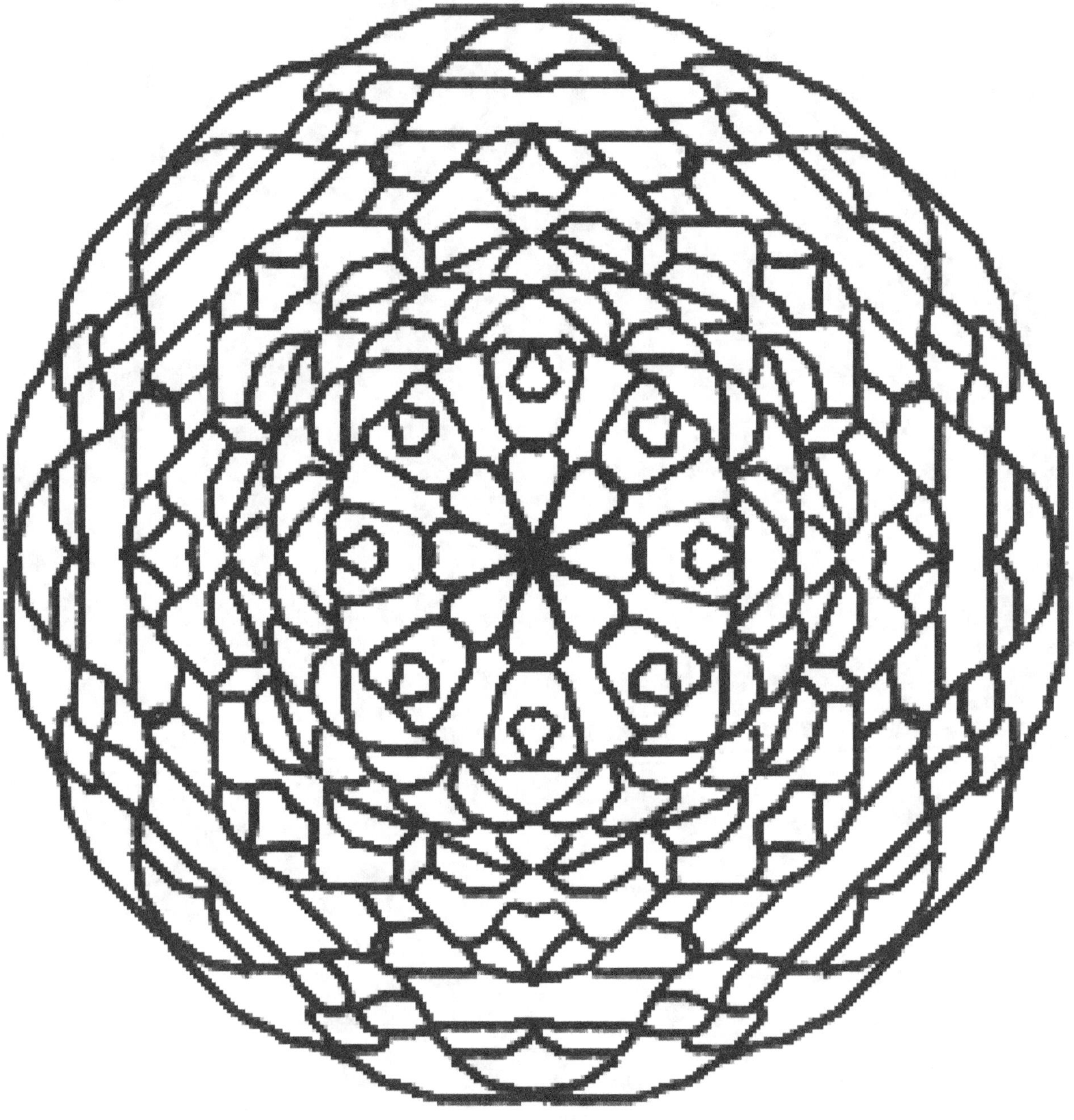

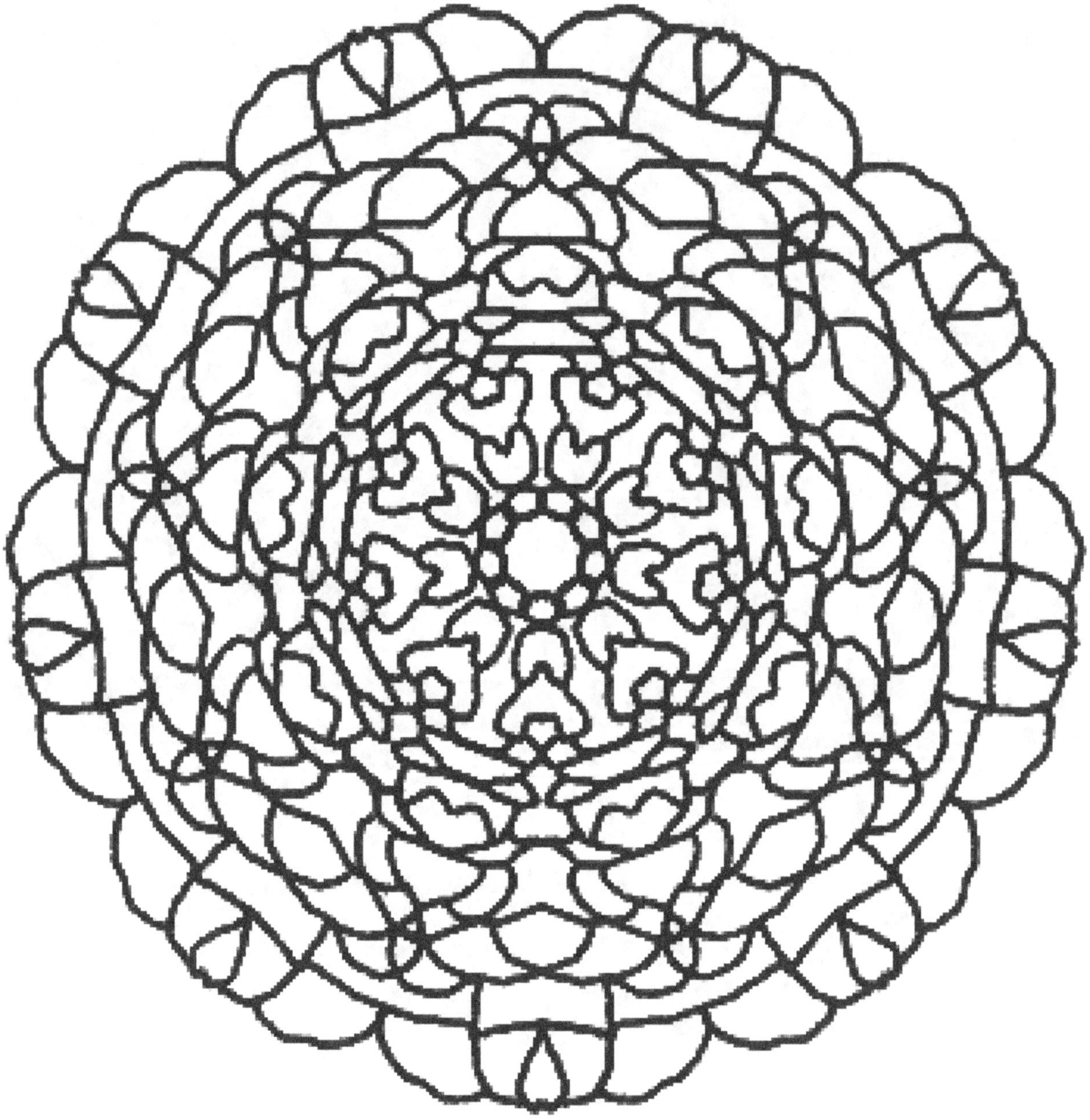

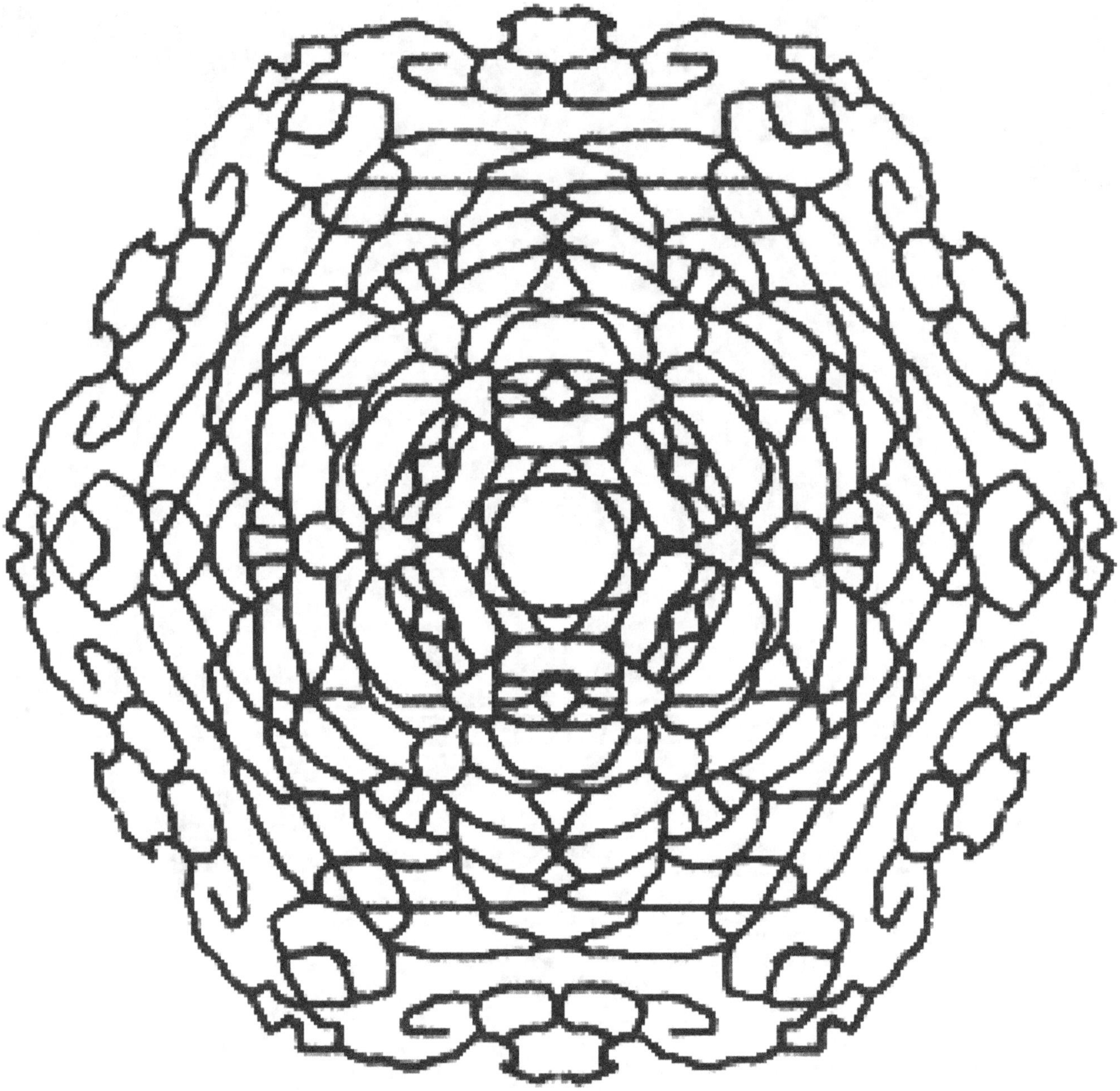

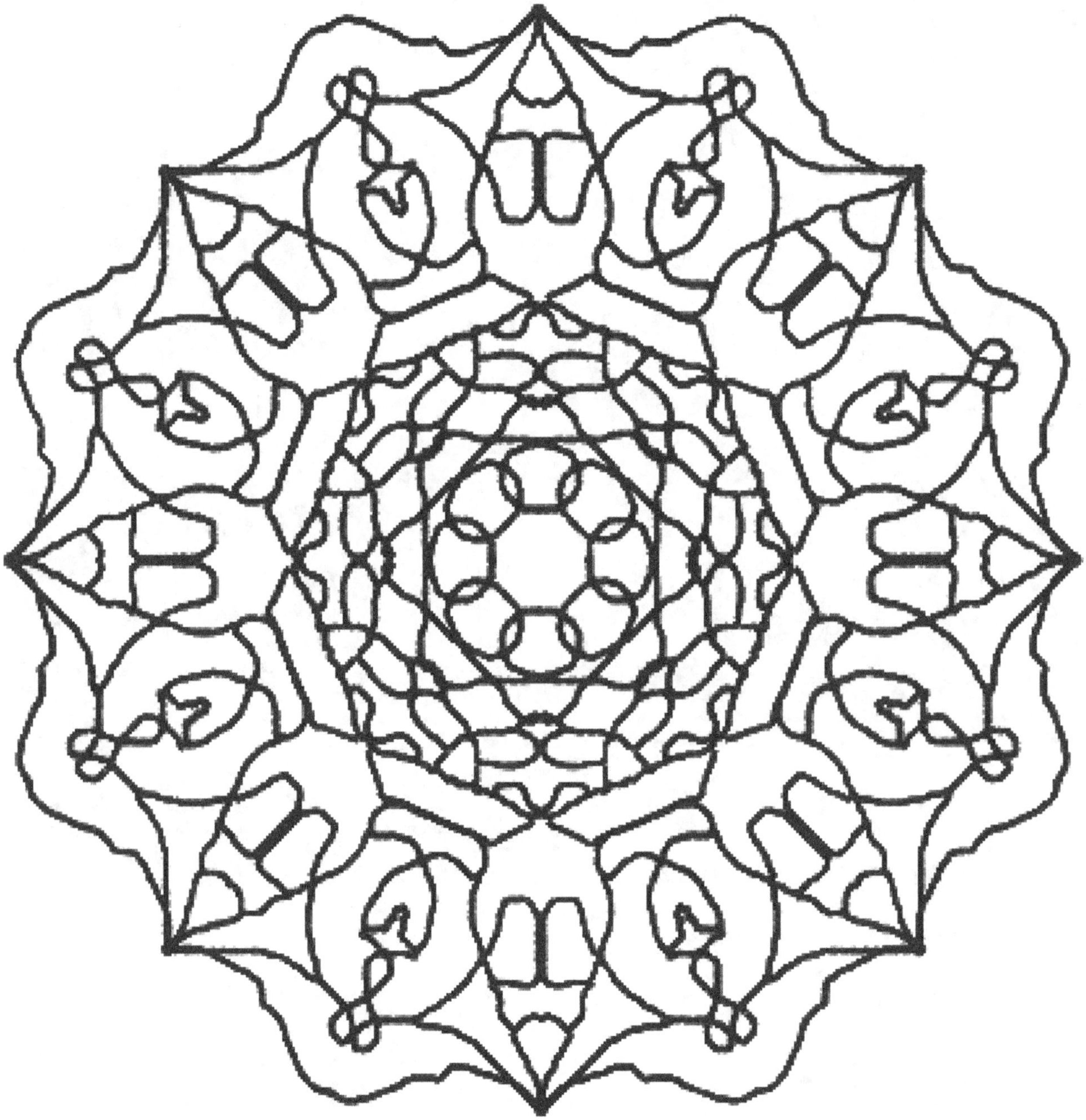

www.ingramcontent.com/pod-product-compliance
Lightning Source LLC
Chambersburg PA
CBHW080628220526
45467CB00011B/3410
* 9 7 9 8 7 1 9 6 0 4 7 6 3 *